Alan Turing: Unlocking the Enigma

David Boyle

First published 2014 by Endeavour Press Ltd.

This edition published 2014 by The Real Press.

The Real Press,

The Red House,

87 Coombe Road,

Steyning,

West Sussex

BN44 3LF

Prologue

'Be it enacted by the Queen's most Excellent Majesty, by and with the advice and consent of the Lords Spiritual and Temporal, and Commons, in this present Parliament assembled, and by the authority of the same, as follows: 1 Statutory Pardon of Alan Mathison Turing.'
Introduction to the draft law, introduced into the House of Lords, July 2013

It was unusually full for a Friday in the House of Lords as the peers gathered just before lunch on 19 July 2013. There, in the venerable red and gold of the Westminster debating chamber, Lord Sharkey – the former advertising executive John Sharkey – proposed a 'private members bill' to give a statutory pardon to one of Britain's greatest scientists, Alan Turing.

Present in the chamber to hear him were members of Turing's family, and at least one former colleague of his at the top secret code breaking establishment at Bletchley Park, where the Nazi Enigma code had been broken during the Second World War. 'Turing's reputation as one of the most brilliant scientists of the twentieth century has grown so much,' said Sharkey, 'that it now seemed extraordinary that he had been hounded for his homosexuality, and in the series of events leading to his suicide in 1954.' More than half a century had gone by since those events, and it was time for the nation to make some amends.

The original campaign for a pardon was the idea of computer scientist John Graham-Cumming, who had begun by calling for an official apology for the way Turing was treated after his conviction. He wrote to the Queen to ask for Turing to be awarded a posthumous knighthood. The campaign won widespread support and, by 2009, Prime Minister Gordon Brown had agreed to apologise. 'While Mr Turing was dealt with under the law of the time and we can't put the clock back, his treatment was of course utterly unfair,' he wrote in the *Daily Telegraph*. 'I am pleased to have the chance to say how deeply sorry I, and we all are, for what happened to him.'

But the campaigners wanted more than just an apology; they wanted a proper pardon. The government refused on the grounds that it would set a precedent, even though pardons had recently been given to 18 former terrorists under the Northern Ireland Agreement and 304 of those shot for cowardice during the First World War. All that could be done, in the face of that refusal, was to change the law.

Sharkey was a Liberal Democrat peer and he had two interests in taking the campaign further. He had been campaigning for a blanket pardon for all the remaining 16,000 living victims of the Labouchère revision to the Criminal Law Amendment Act back in 1885, which had first criminalised homosexual acts, and tried to force the issue in Parliament in 2011. It gave pardons to all those still living who had been convicted, but it excluded those who had died, like Turing and another 59,000 people. Sharkey was advised that the best way forward to extend this would be to engineer a pardon for one of the very greatest of those convicted.

Sharkey's second interest was that he had always been a great admirer of Turing, having studied mathematics at university under Robin Gandy, Turing's great friend and his only PhD student.

So the scene was set for an unusual event.

'My Lords,' said Sharkey, rising to his feet. 'On 6 August 1885, late at night in the Commons debate on the Criminal Law Amendment Act, Henry Labouchère suddenly produced an amendment to the Bill before the House. This amendment criminalised homosexual acts. The only discussion was over the penalty to be imposed. Labouchère had proposed a maximum of one year. Sir Henry James suggested two years and Labouchère agreed. The whole debate had four speakers, including Labouchère. It lasted four minutes and consisted of a total of 440 words, but 75,000 men were convicted under this amendment, and Alan Turing was one of those.'

But it was already clear by then that, whether Sharkey succeeded or failed, Turing's reputation was rising all over the world, and he was increasingly prominent in so many of the most important debates of the early twenty-first century – about the nature of humanity, the possibilities of artificial life, the meaning of human endeavour, and the direction of 'progress'.

Turing had important things to say on all of these, and he is probably best known for his wartime code-cracking, but he ought perhaps to be remembered more for his pioneering contribution to the very beginning of information technology. Partly he had been overlooked until now because of a contention between the supporters of rival American and British claims to have originated computing, and partly because of the self-effacing personality of the man himself. It was also partly because of his early death, two weeks before his 42nd birthday.

But that is changing. Alan Turing appears to be becoming a symbol of the shift towards computing, not least because of his attitude of open-minded defiance of convention and conventional thinking. Not only did he conceptualise the modern computer – imagining a simple machine that could use different programmes – but he put his thinking into practice in the great code breaking struggle with the Nazis in World War II, and followed it up with pioneering early work in the mathematics of biology and chaos.

As if that wasn't enough, he has now assumed the status of a martyr of the modern age, for his logic, his rationalism and his unashamed homosexuality, and for the way he was treated as a result by the forces of the law – and of course because this appears to have led to his suicide.

Turning himself, as one might expect, was a strange mixture of character traits and paradoxes. He was confident in his own abilities, amusing and witty with friends, yet shy and uncertain in company, except with the few people he trusted. He relied on relentless logic, yet also managed an almost mystical ability to intuit mathematical proofs. He combined a rigid clarity and scepticism about human specialness, but he was also fascinated by fairy tales and was famously obsessed with the Disney film *Snow White and the Seven Dwarfs*.

The overwhelming feeling about Turing, from reading accounts of his life – and his mother wrote a detailed tribute after his death – is just how English he was. Many of his fellow countrymen failed to understand him at all, and he worked part of his career with American and German mathematicians at Princeton University, but he was deeply English in his sheer practicality, for the literalism with which he turned intellectual ideas into practical projects. He was a true successor to the great British empiricists, John Locke and David Hume, and the exclusion of every consideration except sense data. It is a theme that keeps returning in his life and work.

My own interest in Turing began when I was writing about the changing meaning of the word 'authenticity', and Turing was a particularly paradoxical figure in this debate. He remains the hero of those who believe that technology will rapidly replace the purely human. Yet there are elements of Turing's multi-faceted personality that it would be possible to hail on the other side – his belief in human possibility, his tolerance and above all his romanticism: one of his closest friends was the future fantasy writer Alan Garner, later the author of *The Weirdstone of Brisingamen*.

But I have always been interested in Turing for another reason too. He was born in the neighbourhood where I was brought up, a Georgian enclave near Paddington Station in London, known for its plane trees, its dubious Edwardian night life and for its network of canals, earning it the title 'Little Venice'.

I

'The criterion which we use to test the genuineness of apparent statements of fact is the criterion of verifiability.'

A.J. Ayer, *Language, Truth and Logic*, 1936

Turing may have been English in the depths of his soul, but he was conceived in the Indian town of Chatrapur, near Madras. His father, Julius Turing, was in the Indian Civil Service. When it was clear that Alan's mother, Sara, was pregnant, the couple came home by ship and he was born in a nursing home in Paddington on 23 June 1912, two months after the *Titanic* went down. He was baptised Alan Mathison Turing under the imposing Victorian spire of St Saviour's Church in Warwick Avenue, and was brought home to live at Warrington Lodge, a stone's throw from the church in Warrington Crescent. He had an elder brother, John.

Warrington Crescent was at the time, and has been for most of its existence, a strange mixture. It remains to this day a Georgian terrace, with gaps caused by bombs from a Zeppelin a few years after the Turing family lived there. At one end are the green, grubby waters of the Regent's Canal; at the other is the flamboyant Warrington Hotel, with its louche painted interior, on the corner of the then notorious red light district of Portland Road (now Randolph Avenue).

Turing was a charming child, making up words like *quockling* (seagulls fighting over food) or *greasicle* (a guttering candle), all details that Sara Turing lovingly records. He found reading difficult to start with, but discovered a copy of a book called *Reading Without Tears* and taught himself in three weeks. For the rest of his life he would always prefer puzzling out problems for himself.

He was always fascinated by numbers and his biographers have pinpointed the moment when he was given a book called *Natural Wonders Every Child Should Know* by Edwin Tenney Brewster.

Brewster was of the generation who believed that the metaphor of a machine was a useful way of describing the relationship between body and mind. Turing clearly took the lesson to heart.

He was bought up by a couple in St Leonards-on-Sea while his parents went back to India and, by the age of nine, had become increasingly withdrawn. His guardians complained about his bookishness. He missed his parents terribly and when they heard about it they had the good sense to remove him from his preparatory school. He was due to go to Sherborne, the famous independent school in Dorset, just as the General Strike broke out in 1926. The railways and public transport broke down and Turing impressed his new teachers by cycling all the way from Southampton, about 60 miles.

His handwriting was atrocious and he was useless at subjects like English and Latin, but he was already obsessed with mathematics, solving problems by going straight for the answer without the intervening calculation. It was an unnerving ability. He calculated Gregor's series for tan $[1]$ $^(x)$ without realising it had been done two centuries before. He asked his teacher if the calculation was correct. Not knowing better, the teacher assumed he had simply copied it out of a book. His housemaster described it as 'trying to build a roof without the foundations'. Teaching him could be a frustrating business, as he always rushed on ahead of the syllabus.

Turing kept a diary which he locked away. Another boy forced the lock and destroyed it. Sherborne was at the time notorious as the setting for Alec Waugh's youthful homosexual novel *The Loom of Youth*, and the diary incident seems to have been linked with blossoming sexuality. In 1928, when he was sixteen, a particularly romantic friendship grew up between Turing and his brilliant contemporary Christopher Morcom. Morcom was a formative influence and, in some ways, the love of his life. The two boys regarded each other as pioneering scientists, determined to interpret the world, but Morcom never fulfilled his promise. He won a place at Trinity College, Cambridge, but died shortly afterwards of tuberculosis.

Turing was prostrated by grief. He wrote to Morcom's mother:

'I feel that I shall meet Morcom again somewhere and that there will be some work for us to do together as there was for us to do here ... it never seems to have occurred to me to make other friends besides Morcom. He made everyone else seem so ordinary.'

Sara Turing also told Morcom's mother that her son was 'treasuring with the tenderness of a woman the pencils and the beautiful star map and other souvenirs you gave him.' Nobody ever took the place of Morcom in his life, but Turing won a place himself at King's College, Cambridge, and went there in 1931, determined somehow to live up to the brilliance and promise of his friend.

*

England is a contradictory place. It has been traditionally one of the most permissive countries in the world for homosexuality, as long as you lived in the right class and the right circles, but paradoxically also one of the most repressive.

The legal shift happened not after the notorious trials of the playwright and socialite Oscar Wilde in 1895, but ten years before, after the so-called Dublin Scandals of 1884. Homosexuality was a charge which the Irish Nationalists flung at the Unionists in the final decades of the nineteenth century. After the brutal murder of the Secretary of State for Ireland, Lord Frederick Cavendish, the constitutional republicans were forced onto the defensive. The homosexuality scare was whipped up by the Nationalist MP for Mallon, William O'Brien, and led to a series of convictions and high-profile acquittals among the Unionist community. It also led to Labouchère's famous amendment to the Criminal Law Amendment Act shortly afterwards.

The origins of the criminalisation of homosexual acts in the tortured politics of Ireland had been forgotten by the time Turing was a student, half a century later. But those around him at King's College were very aware of the care they needed to take. Near his rooms lived the famously gay novelist E. M. Forster, author of *Maurice*. The great economist John Maynard Keynes, also at King's, had carried on a long affair with the artist Duncan Grant. While Turing was studying there, Forster was collecting signatures against the suppression of Radclyffe Hall's lesbian novel *The Well of Loneliness*, which he also thoroughly disliked.

King's was the centre not just of the high-profile Bloomsbury set, but of the influence of the great moral philosopher G. E. Moore, the prophet of moral autonomy. Keynes described Moore's philosophy in terms which Turing would have responded to:

'It was nothing more than the application of logic and rational analysis to the material presented as sense-data. We entirely repudiated a personal liability on us to obey general rules. This was a very important part of our faith, violently and aggressively held.'

'Morality could not be calculated,' said Moore. 'It had to come from within.' It was 'exciting, exhilarating, the beginning of a renaissance, the opening of a new heaven and earth,' wrote Keynes. 'We were the forerunners of a new dispensation; we were not afraid of anything.' Moore's moral ideas dominated the generation that grew up before the First World War, particularly among the influential Bloomsbury set, among whom Keynes was a prominent member. From then on the truth was to be found by intuition as well as reason. This was not the way that Turing was to see the world – though he used his intuition to devastating effect – but it must have influenced him. He was always led by his own intuition before 'general rules'.

Into this exciting and contradictory atmosphere stepped the nineteen-year-old Turing, now reading the left-leaning *New Statesman* and becoming interested in economics, a follower of the proto-Keynesian Arthur Pigou, also then at King's. He was interested, though not passionately, in the peace movement and joined the Anti-War Council, which he described as 'rather communist'. But he was not a socialist; Turing was too much of an individualist for that. He was painfully shy, badly dressed and untidy, not the kind of student who would be invited to meetings of the sophisticated Apostles, the college's famous elite society of intellectuals.

'Alan, as I saw him, made people want to help and protect him though he was rather insulated from human relationships,' wrote Sir Geoffrey Jefferson, the neurologist. 'Or perhaps because of that, we wanted to break through. I personally did not find him easy to get close to.'

Biographers may have over-emphasised Turing's shyness later, but as a student he was clearly strange to people he did not know well. His stammer was irritating and so was his loud crowing laugh. He never quite seemed to meet people's eyes. Not only was he untidy and gauche in his appearance, he also seemed to be indifferent to discomfort. It infuriated his mother his whole life. He always stayed in cheap YMCAs, even when he could afford an upmarket hotel.

He was also sexually aware by then and had begun an on-off relationship with his friend James

Atkins, who asked him to come on a walking holiday in the Lake District in 1933. The weather was hot and Alan sunbathed naked, but his biographers emphasise that neither Atkins, nor any of his successors, managed to take the place of Morcom.

He had also discovered pure mathematics and was powering ahead academically. He did his dissertation on group theory and finished it at the end of 1934. In March 1935 he was elected as a fellow of the college. He was only 22.

II

'All Cretans are liars, as a Cretan poet once told me.'

The original formulation of the liar's paradox by Epimenides the Cretan

One of the most famous paradoxes ever articulated is often known by the title 'the liar's paradox'. At its simplest you can express it just by saying: 'I am lying'. The liar's paradox is a complicated business, discombobulating to think about because after all, if I'm lying, then my statement 'I am lying' must itself be a lie, unless I was actually telling the truth, in which case I would have been telling a lie.

When Turing was a student the liar's paradox was an uncomfortable thorn in the side of the pure mathematicians who were engaged in an international project to secure the philosophical foundations of mathematics. The philosopher Gottfried Leibnitz had believed that the whole of reality could be translated into mathematical symbols and the answers to any disagreements could simply be calculated like mathematical problems.

At the beginning of the century the German philosopher Gottlob Frege was at the time struggling to secure this underpinning. The second volume of his masterwork *Grundgesetze* was ready for publication in 1903, when the King's College philosopher Bertrand Russell wrote to him and punctured a hole in his assumptions. The idea that mathematics could provide a logical underpinning to everything never quite recovered Russell and Frege's joint failure to resolve the contradictions.

Worse, the great academic struggle in mathematics in those days was not just about formal logic; it also seemed at the time to have implications for international politics. The followers of David Hilbert who were struggling to solve the paradoxes at the heart of the foundations of the science believed that this was a project that could underpin internationalism. Frege's opinions verged on the proto-fascist, but Hilbert and others believed this could lead to a more secure foundation for international understanding, and potentially therefore for peace.

The trouble was that the new generation were rejecting this ambition, just as the Cambridge Apostles had rejected the idea that you could somehow calculate right and wrong. Then, in 1931, the Austrian mathematician Kurt Gödel showed that mathematics could not be used to prove itself consistent or complete. It torpedoed Frege's great internationalist project once and for all, but it also allowed for new thinking to emerge. It was known as the Incompleteness Theorem.

Turing was coming into his own during these debates, and he was particularly interested in the liar's paradox, or the *Entscheidnugsproblem*. The question that lay before Turing and his contemporaries was not so much whether or not the *Entscheidnugsproblem* could be solved or resolved in some way mathematically, but whether a solution could be attained at all, by any other means.

Turing took up long-distance running during that summer when he was first a fellow of the college and it helped him to think. Relaxing after one of these runs, out to the village of Grantchester – the scene of all those summer afternoons on the river a generation before with Rupert Brooke and his friends from the Apostles – an idea struck him. What if there was some kind of machine capable of working out the *Entscheidnugsproblem*?

This was the germ of the idea that eventually became a computer, but no such thing existed at the time. There were mechanical calculators in most accounting officers, which would add, subtract, divide and multiply on demand. There were slide rules for undertaking more complicated calculations. The basics of computing had long since been conceptualised by the Victorian Charles Babbage, inventor of the analytical machine, helped by Byron's daughter Ada Lovelace, who invented an engine that could weave maths patterns like a loom.

Looms are an important inspiration for modern computers because weaving required punchcards which would instruct the machine to weave in certain patterns, and this was the kind of system that Turing imagined – though his friend Robin Gandy said later that Turing had never heard of the Babbage machine.

Turing imagined a machine that could carry out a calculation or apply an algorithm. Next, he said, imagine that you had a universal machine that could carry out all the possible algorithms, using a series of different cards like the looms do. Now, could you use the universal machine to work out if the *Entscheidnugsproblem* could be calculated? The answer, said Turing, was you couldn't: he had produced a rigorous mathematical proof that some problems were undecidable.

The following year, through the excitement of the Berlin Olympics, Turing worked on his paper. It was called 'On computable numbers, with an application to the *Entscheidnugsproblem*.' He showed the very first draft to his tutor, Max Newman. Newman was sceptical at first but changed his mind and was soon urging Turing to publish it. It was published early in 1937 in the proceedings of the London Mathematical Society.

The result was a mathematical proof that some mathematical problems are simply unsolvable, on the grounds that they will not be solved by any definite process. Turing had used his machines as a novel mathematical tool. It was a confirmation of Gödel's work, but using a highly original approach – involving a leap of imagination to provide mathematical clarity. The great advantage of imagining a machine to do the work was that it made the question of whether the calculation was too complex for a human being quite irrelevant. 'Human memory is necessarily limited,' he wrote. His Turing machines could potentially see if big numbers are the same at a glance, something that would be quite impossible for human beings.

But Turing's paper suggested a theoretical machine, a metaphor designed to frame the argument in such a way that it could be proved mathematically. He was not imagining at this stage that an actual machine might be built like that. Yet there is also an element of what would eventually be the Turing Test, and it stems from the positivism that prevailed at the time through the philosophical departments of Europe. Turing's paper asserted that the reality of the world can be defined by what is possible for a machine.

'Although perfectly sound', he wrote, '...[the argument] has the disadvantage that it may leave the reader with the feeling that "there must be something wrong".' This is true, but Turing was talking about a specific mathematical function 'decidability' or, as became clear, 'computability'.

On the other hand, he did make a big step towards the practical creation of a Turing machine by proposing that the binary system should be used, once again based on the kind of punchcards that programme a loom – where the holes were either there or not. Even as he drafted the paper, he was talking to his friend David Champernowne, the mathematician, about whether it might be possible to build a universal machine. Champernowne said you would need a building the size of London's Royal Albert Hall. As it turned out, he was wrong.

*

It is one of the peculiarities of human endeavour that breakthroughs often take place simultaneously, and it so happened that – just as Turing was coming round to the idea of publishing his own paper – the Princeton mathematician Alonzo Church published a paper on *definability*, which was very close to Turing's *computability*. Struck by the similarities, Newman wrote to Church and asked if Turing could go to Princeton and study with him. Newman was already concerned about Turing's isolation. He was afraid that Turing's habit of studying alone and wrestling with problems by himself might slow him down. He needed to work alongside people.

Yet Church was also a loner, and even more of one than Turing. He has been described as looking like 'a cross between a panda and a large owl', and had the habit of talking very slowly in complete and flawless sentences, as if he was reading out of a book. If he was interrupted there would be an awkward silence as he tried to recover himself. Church had a habit of working all night and was well-known for his peculiar habits. He would arrive late for departmental tea, pouring the milk into the teapot, stirring it around and then drinking the mixture. In his lectures he would spend the first ten minutes in silence washing the blackboard, then, still in silence, he would wait until it dried. He was not necessarily the gregarious companion that Turing needed.

Even so, Turing went. In September 1936 Sara Turing saw her son off at Southampton on the Cunard liner *Berengaria*. He bought with him an old sextant and a battered violin he had bought in the flea markets in London's Farringdon Road. A week later he was alone in America.

It was a thrilling time to be in Princeton. The Institute of Advanced Study already included Albert

Einstein on its faculty and was emerging as one of the main routes out of Nazi Germany for academic Jewish refugees. The head of Turing's new department was the sophisticated John von Neumann, and Turing found himself taken up by him, invited to parties and forced in socialising. The American newspapers were full of the affair between the new king Edward VIII and an American divorcee called Wallis Simpson, the basic facts of which were still being suppressed by the British press. It was as if America gave Turing a glimpse of the way the world really was.

For all his foibles, Church boosted Turing's career by a powerfully supportive review in the *Journal of Symbolic Logic*, during which he coined the phrase 'Turing Machines'. Their work is now usually combined under the heading the *Church-Turing Thesis*.

Princeton was a success for Turing and, at the end of the year, von Neumann offered him a fellowship at $2,000 a year and Turing accepted, though he went back to England in the summer for his twenty-fifth birthday. He was already thinking more broadly about computers and especially their use in creating codes. His contemporary at MIT, Claude Channon, had described an encoding machine which used Boolean algebra to translate messages into a number and to multiply the number by another huge and secret number before transmitting it. The principle was that solving this code should take a hundred years working eight hours a day on desk calculations. Turing had begun to wonder whether his machines could drive this process further.

When his own article was finally published he gave his mother an offprint. She wrote notes in the margin, 'one against what I understood, another to denote what with further explanation I might grasp, while the third mark indicated what no power on earth could make me comprehend'.

Even so, working with Church was not rewarding. Turing's awkwardness came from shyness, but there was more than a little of the Asperger's about Church. So in 1938 Turing turned down another offer, to be von Neumann's assistant. The war clouds were gathering in Europe over the issue of the Sudetenland, and Turing wanted to be home. Once there he applied to the Royal Society for a grant to build a machine to calculate the number of zeroes in the Riemann zeta function. They gave him £40 and his Cambridge rooms filled slowly with gear wheels, but his heart was barely in it.

It was during this period, in the countdown to war, that he had two crucial encounters. The first of these was with Ludwig Wittgenstein, the great Austrian philosopher who had taken over the Cambridge chair of philosophy vacated by Moore in 1937. Wittgenstein had given away a fortune inherited from his father and he was known also for his complete lack of small talk – and for originating not just one but two contradictory and ground-breaking contributions to the philosophy of mind. Turing found him fascinating:

'His face was lean and brown, his profile aquiline and strikingly beautiful, his head was covered with a curly mass of brown hair. I observed the respectful attention that everyone in the room paid to him ... his look was concentrated, he made striking gestures with his hands as if he was discoursing. All the others maintained an intent and respectful silence.'

Wittgenstein lectured in his own room in an old lumber jacket without any notes or preparation, and with copious periods of lengthy silence. When he did read from notes, he told his biographer Norman Malcolm, the words 'come out like corpses'. Turing was the only mathematician there and soon the lectures turned into a conversation between the two men, testing Wittgenstein's assertion that common sense trumped logic. For Wittgenstein, the liar's paradox was a 'useless language game'. Turing claimed it *did* matter because a practical project could use mathematics which had been compromised by it. The bridge they were building could fall down.

We know something about the conversations between two of the great thinkers of the century because they were recorded in detailed notes and reconstructed into a dialogue that was published in 1976. As the only mathematician Turing had to face the full brunt of Wittgenstein's scepticism – especially when it came to the business of the liar's paradox. Why does it matter, asks Wittgenstein?

'What puzzles one is that one usually uses a contradiction as a criterion for having done something wrong, but in this case one cannot find anything done wrong.'

'Yes – and more,' says Wittgenstein. 'Nothing has been done wrong ... where will the harm come?'

'The real harm,' says Turing, 'will not come in unless there is an application, in which a bridge may fall down or something of that sort.'

It was important because it was precisely Wittgenstein's accusation – taking logic too far from common sense – which Turing was to be accused of by later generations. The question before them was how much these logical peculiarities mattered in the real world. Wittgenstein denied that they did. Turing bravely stuck to his position. He would return to the same argument a decade later.

Turing's second encounter sounds silly in comparison, but it was important to Turing and is usually emphasised by his biographers. It was with Walt Disney's great breakthrough in cartoon cinematography, *Snow White and the Seven Dwarfs*. This was released in 1937 and Turing went to see it with his friend David Champernowne, and was completely overwhelmed. It is interesting that mathematicians tended to be fascinated by the film: Gödel was also obsessed with it. But it was the scene with the poisoned apple that he found particularly compelling:

'*Dip the apple in the brew;*

Let the sleeping death seep through.'

Turing took to reciting verses of this scene to himself. He stayed fascinated with the film for the rest of his life.

But the events leading to war were now accelerating. News of Turing's interest in codes had reached Commander Alastair Denniston, the director of the British government's new Code and Cipher School. Denniston was collecting anyone with interest or skills in codes, from mathematicians to crossword puzzle experts. Turing was an obvious expert to approach.

III

'It is a riddle wrapped in a mystery inside an enigma.'

Winston Churchill's speech on Russia, 1939

It was the first action in the war at sea. A few hours after the declaration of war between Germany, Britain and France, the German submarine U-30, under Captain Fritz-Julius Lemp, torpedoed and sank the Cunard liner *Athenia*, with the loss of 117 lives. 20 months later Lemp's submarine (U-110) was on the surface, forced into the open by the British destroyer *Bulldog*. The crew were in the water, being picked up, and a small boat from the *Bulldog* with an armed boarding party was alongside the stricken submarine.

Led by a sub-lieutenant called David Balme the boarding party managed to climb through the damaged conning tower, aware that U-110 might sink beneath them at any moment, and found the control room deserted. The sailors spread through the submarine with orders to seize any charts and books that were not novels. The telegraphist in the group went straight to the signals office and grabbed the signal logs and paybooks, which seemed to have been abandoned.

To his astonishment there in front of him was an elusive Enigma coding machine, still plugged in. The telegraphist fiddled with it, didn't understand it and so sent it down the chain of men up the hatch. When the naval authorities realised what it was they had found the machine was rushed to the top secret code centre at Bletchley Park. It was a major breakthrough in the struggle to crack the elusive Nazi naval code, and Turing, as a temporary civil servant in the Foreign Office Department of Communications, was at the heart of the British organisation devised to crack it.

This was not the first Enigma machine the British had taken into their possession. They had been given one by the Poles at the beginning of the war.

They had also captured another. But even before the war they had recognised the critical importance of cracking the Enigma code, and naval Enigma was far more difficult to solve. That was the prime focus of the strange mixture of individuals who joined Turing at Bletchley, a mock Tudor pile deliberately chosen by the head of secret intelligence, Captain Quex Sinclair, because it was on the railway line midway between the two ancient university towns of Oxford and Cambridge.

Throughout the war, under huge stress and some discomfort, the government's secret code breakers lived in ever-greater numbers at Bletchley, and the captured code books and the occasional captured coding machine were rushed there, sometimes so fast from a crashed plane that the blood stains on the code book were still wet.

At the outbreak of war Turing had converted his considerable savings into two large silver ingots, which he buried in a wood near Shenley, slipping a disk as he lifted them into a pram for the task (he never managed to find them again). He arrived at

Bletchley in a small group, under the usual code of 'Captain Ridley's Shooting Party', on 4 September 1939. He and three colleagues were lodged temporarily in a low building next to the big house called The Cottage before he moved into rooms in the Crown pub in Shenley Brooke End. There he was looked after by the landlady Mrs Ramshaw, who constantly scolded him about his dishevelled appearance.

The next few years proved to be the busiest and arguably most important period of Turing's short life, although he would be largely unknown by the general public, and little known even in the military intelligence circles. He wasn't alone: around him were not just mathematicians and crossword experts, but linguists, statisticians, puzzle creators, and strange individuals from the future novelist Angus Wilson to the future Home Secretary Roy Jenkins, and the future historian Asa Briggs, all of them in their own enclosed huts, revealing nothing to the outside world and little to each other. There were Egyptologists, bridge players, and even one expert on seaweeds and mosses who had been sent there because of a misunderstanding of the biological term 'cryptogams', and who played a critical role working out how to dry out code books damaged by sea water.

The historian Hugh Trevor Roper, who visited often, described the atmosphere as 'friendly informality verging on apparent anarchy'. One military policeman famously mistook Bletchley for a military asylum.

Turing and his colleagues were not starting from scratch. Behind them were centuries of work on code breaking, primarily the great insight by Turing's Victorian predecessor Charles Babbage, who realised that the way to treat codes was to imagine the letters were random. If they *were* random every letter would be used an average number of times, and then whatever is not average in the coded passage is a potential clue.

Yet Enigma was a huge challenge. It looked like a typewriter, but with no space for paper. It had lights for each letter and, inside it, the three rotors (and later more than three) could be arranged in a range of different ways, each one linked to a different set of electrical connections. The key code, with the rotor setting, would be in a three letter key for each day, which all the machine operators would look up in the code book. It was believed to be impregnable. The three rotors could mean more than 17,000 different solutions for a given message, but – since the three rotors could be rearranged in any of six different ways – the number of combinations reached over 105,000.

But here again Turing and colleagues could rely on the previous breakthroughs by the Polish mathematicians who had been able to read Enigma messages for some time, by using the system's weaknesses. For one thing, it would have to go through all 26 positions before the middle rotor moved, which meant you knew that the first 26 letters of any message only used one rotor. There was also the fatal mistake made by the German military of the three letter key setting usually being sent twice and you knew there would be a link between the first and fourth letters and so on (this stopped in May 1940).

The Poles, led by the mathematicians Jerzy Rozycki, Henryk Zygalski and Marian Rejewski, had used a system of paper with punched holes with all the possible combinations and shone lights through from below, shifting the papers around until one light shone all the way through. They called this system, and the machine that helped them, the *bombe*. It was to link up with Turing's own ideas about computing.

By the outbreak of war the code breakers at Bletchley had some advantages. They were soon able to recognise the codes of origin for each message, and – despite the short supply of coloured pencils – they began to code them visually, yellow for the Norwegian campaign, green for the army, red for the Luftwaffe. This was the situation when Turing arrived there and was given the task of overseeing the theoretical aspects of cracking the coded messages. He was soon known as 'The Prof'.

In the early weeks of the war he spent his time writing out in an almost illegible longhand a plan for cracking the codes, working the whole process out logically. The key point was that Coded Enigma messages were reversible, and – since they were reversible – they could reverse the process which the machine went through. The question was: how? Turing was sent out soon afterwards to Paris to meet a group of Polish code breakers, nearly causing the furious resignation of the senior cryptographer Dillwyn Knox, because he was taking the precious Polish *bombe* sheets out of the country.

Turing was clear that they would need two elements. The first was a series of what he called cribs, bits of code that were likely-looking translations. The second was a much improved, much faster version of the Polish *bombe* – a machine for testing out the various cribs to see if they worked, without which the whole process would be impossibly time-consuming. Speed was always vital at Bletchley Park.

The first problem to solve was the cribs. There were clues. Sometimes it was clear that some messages were weather reports. Sometimes the words 'weather' or 'Heil Hitler!' were obvious. One signaller was in the habit of ending his signals 'nothing to report' (*nicht zu melden*). But it was Turing's colleague John Herival who provided the best route for cribs. He was dozing by the fire and woke up with a start, imagining himself as a German signal officer with an Enigma machine, and suddenly realised that laziness would mean they would often just use the same settings as the day before. Straight away he began to work out how to detect when they did.

Then there was the problem of a crib testing machine. This time it was not enough to imagine the kind of computing machine that might solve the problem. Turing and his colleague Gordon Welchman (from Hut 6) had to actually build one. His first *bombe* was called Victory. It was seven feet long and six feet high, and it weighed a ton. It had the power to simulate the actions of 30 Enigma machines at once. It also leaked oil, was constantly getting itself jammed, and gave people electric shocks.

Victory was built in Letchworth by the British Tabulating Machine Company under their chief engineer, Doc Keen. Once it was ready there was a major problem of how to get it to Bletchley Park. The huge security it required would, the authorities thought, simply draw attention to it. In the end it was sent, quite openly, on the back of a lorry. It was installed in Hut 1 on 18 March 1940, just days before the invasion of Norway.

There is a *bombe* in the preserved Hut 8 at Bletchley to this day, but it is only a replica. None of the working machines have survived, though 200 of them were eventually built, operated mainly by Wrens (women naval personnel) at sites in north London like Eastcote and Stanmore.

Once the Phoney War was over and Victory was in place a rhythm began to emerge. When the first few messages emerged with the key settings for that day they were sent to Hut 8, where a friend of

Turing's from Princeton called Shaun Wylie searched for phrases that might be repeated, or obvious proper names. When his cribs began to pile up they would go to the machine room. It was stressful work, which had to be carried out quickly and accurately. One wire out of place on the *bombe* would mean a short circuit and that would put them back for hours. Then the machine would stop when it reached a contradiction or an answer and the settings would be checked until it stopped at an answer which seemed to produce obvious German.

Then it would go over to Hut 3, where the message would be translated, mostly by particularly meticulous former schoolmasters, interpreted and sent out. Then the machine would be stripped down and given the next task. And so it would go on, far into the night.

There was an unmilitary atmosphere of informality combined with seriousness. Nobody wore uniforms. Absolute discretion was vital in case the word leaked out, via a hint to families for example, that would allow the Nazis to know their messages were being read. The food was terrible, full of watery cabbage and stale fat. There was a shortage of nearly everything, except perhaps musicians. Madrigals were sung by the canal on summer evenings.

Turing failed to quite fit in at Bletchley. Bletchley alumni remember him as a 'bit of a weirdo', walking quickly along the paths around the estate, looking worried. On one occasion he was arrested by the local police because he looked suspicious, and – when he was taken to the police station – he was found not to have signed his identity card. He claimed, in his typically literal way, that he had taken seriously the rule that you were not supposed to write on them. It was precisely that kind of contradiction that frustrated him. Turing also bothered his superiors. The precise balance of admiration and irritation was expressed in a letter about him written by Knox:

'He is very difficult to anchor down. He is very clever, but quite irresponsible and throws out a mass of suggestions of all degrees of merit. I have just, but only just, enough authority and ability to keep him and his ideas in some sort of order and discipline, but he is very nice about it all.'

*

Once the Battle of Britain was over and the Battle of the Atlantic was taking shape, early in 1941, Turing and his team were forced to focus on the continuing problem of Naval Enigma.

This was much more difficult. The German Navy used an adjustable reflector fixed in 26 different positions on their machines. Instead of using a coded three-letter key, they used two three-letter keys with extra random letters for each one, arranged on top of each other in four pairs of letters. Every time any of these elements changed, or another rotor was added, they had to go back to the drawing board at Bletchley.

The code breakers had been able to read the Norwegian campaign signals by April 1940 and the Luftwaffe messages had become readable just when they were most needed during the Battle of Britain, though it was still not quite clear how to tell senior military officers about this intelligence without either breaking the secret of Enigma, or failing to convey the fact that this was hardly a piece of tittle-tattle, but genuine information. But Naval Enigma remained enigmatic.

Frank Birch, the head of the German naval section at Bletchley, was particularly frustrated. 'Hut 8 ... hasn't produced any results at all so far ... Turing and Twinn are brilliant, but like many brilliant people, they are not practical. They are untidy, they lose things, they can't copy out right, and dither between theory and cribbing. Neither do they have the determination of practical men.'

What he really needed was books of tables so when the Enigma machine was captured from U-110 it was a turning point. Turing had backed a foolhardy plan by the future novelist Ian Fleming to pretend to be a ditched German pilot, and to capture the patrol boat sent to rescue him, but this had very sensibly been cancelled. A four-rotor Enigma machine was captured from U-559, plus the mysterious *Shark* code key book in October 1942, and two British seamen sank with the submarine in the act of getting it out, but U-110 was the breakthrough. By then Turing was deeply engaged because, as he put it, 'no one else was doing anything about it and I could have it to myself'.

Turing was now a familiar figure around Bletchley Park. He wore a gas mask on his bike to avoid the pollen. He famously chained his mug to a radiator and used string to hold up his trousers. He was often unshaven and – even more peculiar in a semi-military world – found knitting in a corner. He was briefly a member of the Home Guard, but got bored of it in 1942 and stopped turning up. The commander tried to frighten him with military law, only to find that on his application form under the question: 'do you understand that by enrolling in the Home Guard you place yourself liable to military law?' Turing had written 'No'.

One of the new elements for Turing, from the all-male worlds of Sherborne and King's, was the presence of large numbers of women, mainly Wrens who operated the machines and other personnel drafted in from the nearby corset factory. All he told his mother about Bletchley was that he had a hundred girls working under him. One of them amazed the others by determinedly greeting him on Christmas Day with: 'A happy Christmas, Alan'.

'They held him in great awe,' wrote Sara Turing later, 'largely because, when he rushed into their part of the building on business, he never gave the least indication that he even noticed them. The truth probably is that he was equally alarmed by them.'

In fact, one of the female mathematicians was becoming close to Turing: Joan Clarke, who was also working on the naval Enigma code. They became friends, went to the cinema and spent their leaves together, meeting each other's parents. Soon they were engaged and Turing confided to her that he had 'homosexual tendencies'. She was unfazed. In the summer of 1941 they went on a cycling holiday and, when they came back to Bletchley, Turing told her they should break the engagement.

*

Turing may have been eccentric, and extremely shy, but he was not incompetent with people, as some biographers have suggested. Nor was he too shy to organise a letter to Winston Churchill spelling out the things they badly needed, which was taken to Downing Street by a colleague who – in true Bletchley style – forgot his ID card. The letter eventually got through and Churchill wrote on it: 'Make sure they have all they want on extreme priority and report to me that this has been done.'

It was Turing who the authorities chose to send to meet the American code breakers after the USA entered the war, and to make friends with them, which is proof of his ability to engage people. It is true that this was partly because they wanted to ease him out of a management position at Bletchley Park, because – despite his brilliance – he was no manager. But there is no way they would have risked sending him as an emissary to the USA if he was incapable of engaging in social situations.

So it was that Turing was sent on the new liner *Queen Elizabeth*, racing unescorted at 30 knots across the Atlantic, with a special permit from the White House to go anywhere in the American cryptography operation and to help where he could.

V

'I desire the company of a man who could sympathize with me, whose eyes would reply to mine... gentle yet courageous, possessed, has a cultivated as well as a capacious mind, whose tastes are like my own to approve or amend my plans.'

Mary Shelley, *Frankenstein*, 1819

Sailing to the USA changed Turing's life. He was sent to make friends and he did so, finding that the eclectic approach to code breaking adopted by the British was not quite what he found in the USA. Instead of the peculiar mixture of mathematicians and puzzlers, he found a group of lawyers – who were rather cross that, although the British were sharing Turing, they were not sharing his *bombe* machines.

With Turing's help they designed their own. He also visited Bell Laboratories, where their version of the *bombes* used telephone relays instead of rotating drums to imitate each rotor, which meant their settings could be changed at the flick of a switch. The Bell technicians were also looking at ways to code speech more effectively, which fascinated Turing. At Bell his slightly gauche manner was not simply ignored, as it was in England. Colleagues complained that he gave them no sign of recognition when he passed them in the corridors. Turing was horrified; he explained that this was how people behaved in Cambridge and promised to do better. His friends included Claude Shannon at MIT, the American 'Father of Information Theory', with whom he had what turned out to be a historic discussion about whether it might be possible to build a machine to imitate the human brain.

America also broadened his view of sexuality. Turing was propositioned in a hotel by a man in New York City. It isn't clear whether or not he accepted, but perhaps it hardly matters: the point was that he was learning, dangerously perhaps, that he need not hide his sexuality so assiduously.

While Turing was in America in the summer of 1942 his old teacher Max Newman arrived at Bletchley Park to help work on the project they knew as *Fish*. These were the signals generated by a new German code machine called Lorenz, and – like Turing before him – Newman realised they would need a machine to break the code. Here the elements that would eventually coalesce as post-war computer projects were coming together. From Hut 11, which the Bletchley crew knew as the 'Newmanry', Newman managed to bring in help from the Telecommunications Research Establishment at Malvern, and the Post Office Research Station at Dollis Hill in north London.

Perhaps this is not something that Turing, the great loner, would have done. He far preferred wrestling with problems alone and from first principles. But it meant that, when Turing returned to Bletchley in the summer of 1943, his arrival coincided with that of Newman's Colossus machine. It had been designed partly by Tommy Flowers, an electronics engineer from Dollis Hill and it included 1,500 electronic valves. It used to catch fire and tear the printer tapes, but it worked. It was also arguably the first digital electronic computer.

It also meant that there was no place for Turing in the Newmanry now that the conceptual work had been done. Nor was his old position still available. It had been taken over by the chess champion Hugh Alexander, along with the naval Enigma work. In any case, Bletchley was already overcrowded. The new *bombes* had been farmed out around London's suburbs and it made sense for Turing to go elsewhere, so he was sent ten miles away to Hanslope Park, to Special Communications Unit No 3, to carry on the work that he had begun at the Bell Labs on enciphering speech. His assistant Robin Gandy won the prize for naming the new project 'Delilah'.

It was during this period, temporarily attached to a military unit, that he astonished his colleagues at a regimental sports day by entering the long distance race and winning it. For the rest of his life he carried on long-distance running, though an injury prevented him from competing in the run-up to the 1948 London Olympics (the gold medal in the marathon was only seven minutes faster than Turing's best).

Turing seemed to have come back from America much more confident about his sexuality, though he also seemed to have suggested to Joan Clarke that they renew their engagement. She turned him down. But it is possible to get an insight into the way he was thinking about sexuality by his frequent conversations about it, entirely unashamed and brave for the times, including one explosive argument that followed a discussion with his assistant Don Bayley. These were not just conversations either, but a search for a kind of human code which might unlock sexual truths.

The world outside Bletchley was more formal. He moved out of the Crown Inn, via an officers' mess, to a cottage with a kitchen garden with Gandy and a cat called Timothy. He always hated pretending. His conversations were therefore heroically open about sex. Why was Don Bayley outraged? Perhaps because they were not just about being honest; they were also probing conversation seeking out the human equivalent of cribs. 'Sometimes you're sitting talking to someone and you know that in three quarters of an hour you will either be having a marvellous night or you will be kicked out of the room,' he told Gandy later. The sexual code had to be correct.

It also explains something of Turing's approach to machines. The human 'rules', as he described them, were difficult for him. He could not stand pompous people, and rarely did the correct thing, as his mother constantly complained. But neither did he find the normal, polite, coded exchanges between human beings very clear, even about everyday things. He failed to completely understand them and never really respected them. The thinking machines that were to dominate his next decade or so held out an enticing prospect: machines that might take a more logical, sensible approach – perhaps even a more human one – than the complex morass of rules and subtexts that he grappled with in company.

So when Delilah was up and running by the end of the war in 1945, and the Post Office was no longer interested in it, Turing realised that his own interest had moved on as well. He was interested, above all else, in the thinking machine he had discussed with Shannon. In June 1945, after the end of the War in Europe, he accepted a post as temporary senior scientific officer at the National Physical Laboratory at Teddington under Sir Charles Darwin, the grandson of the more famous evolution pioneer. Darwin was dedicated to the great task of preventing the USA getting a head start in the new field of computing – aware that the Americans already had a working model, the Pennsylvania Electrical Numerical Integrator ENIAC, using over 17,000 valves.

ENIAC was not a universal machine as envisaged in Turing's paper before the war. If you wanted to change its function you would have to lay about it with a screwdriver. But his old mentor at Princeton, John von Neumann, was proposing something along the lines of a Turing machine. It was called EDVAC (Electronic Discrete Variable Automatic Computer) and was able to do more than one task using a huge memory, just as Turing proposed.

Turing seems not to have minded that von Neumann's proposal omitted to mention him as the precursor. But he did then propose his own version, ACE (Automatic Computing Engine). His proposal valued the prototype at £11,200. The idea was that it would 'tackle whole problems':

'Instead of repeatedly using human labour for taking material out of the machine and putting it back in at the appropriate moment, all this will be looked after by the machine itself.'

ACE was an important step forward. What made it different was that Turing was wrestling with the same key problem that he had been taught to wrestle with at Bletchley Park: *speed*. To be as effective as he wanted the machine would need a big memory, and there lay the problem. You could hardly use magnetic or punched tape because the machine would take far too long to search it from end to end. Something else would be required and – if the machine was going to do many different programmes and tasks – it would have to be simple. That meant it had to be digital, just 0 and 1. In fact Turing said it was more important that it should be digital than electronic.

If it was fast and simple the machine could 'be made to do any job that could be done by a human computer and ... in one ten-thousandth of the time,' he said. Turing was also imagining a machine that could genuinely 'learn', as he explained in a lecture to the London Mathematical Society in February 1947:

'It would be like a pupil who had learnt much from his master, but had added much more by his own work. When this happens, I feel that one is obliged to regard the machine as showing intelligence.'

These are not metaphors, he said, and here was the start of the continuing debate around the Turing

Test and all that followed. The lecture reveals him imagining the machine being able to take over functions of machine minders and programmers, replacing them with 'mechanical and electrical limbs and sense organs'.

It is important to understand how isolated Turing felt at the time. He was conjuring up a vision of a machine which he could create, realising at the same time that it might one day pose a risk to humanity if it carried on learning, but also identifying with the machine he has conceived. The story of *Frankenstein* has other connotations, but there are parallels with Mary Shelley's famous novel. Here was Turing, imagining that he could create life and immediately defending it, even identifying with it, especially over this question about intelligence. 'I would say fair play to the machine,' he said, defending it from the logical fork that because it is not infallible, it cannot learn. Quite the reverse, said Turing: that is what learning is all about. 'In other words then,' he said, 'if a machine is expected to be infallible, it cannot also be intelligent.'

By then Darwin had been convinced, if not entirely impressed, when Turing spoke about his proposal to the laboratory's executive committee. He was too technical and lost his audience, but he was given £10,000 anyway and told to get on with it. Darwin proudly announced the project in a radio broadcast:

'Turing, who is now on our staff, is showing us how to make his idea come true. Broadly we reckon that it will be possible to do arithmetic a hundred times as fast as a human computer.'

It was the beginning of a fascination with the idea of an 'electronic brain' in the popular press. But it would all take time. Despite the emphasis on speed, the ACE project dragged infuriatingly. It was another four years before the pilot machine was ready, and by then Turing had moved his ideas on.

VI

*'There is something at work in my soul, which I
do not understand.'*

Mary Shelley, *Frankenstein*, 1819

Turing's period with the National Physical Laboratory, and with Darwin, was deeply frustrating. He struggled against the huge class division that emerged between theory and engineering. He was disappointed in the progress towards ACE and irritated that the rules prevented him from getting involved in practical engineering. He left his work at the Laboratory in 1947, on half pay, and took up his fellowship at King's College, which he had set aside eight years before to help crack wartime codes.

Post-war King's was a different place. Keynes was dead. Forster still occupied his rooms, scribbling away. Wittgenstein was ill (he would die of prostate cancer in 1951). The pre-war atmosphere of leftist excitement had given way to a dour, austerity-driven fear of communism. The Cold War was at its height and there was also a new intolerance abroad, a fear of betrayal and with it a terror of what society regarded as 'perversion'. There was also a new prurient interest in what people got up to in the privacy of their bedrooms.

Turing had always been immune to this kind of social control. He remained explicit about his homosexuality, except of course with his mother, who had years of frustration behind her about his failure to behave in precisely the right way. He began a relationship with Neville Johnson, a third-year mathematics student, which was more like 'friendship with sex'. He played chess with Pigou, the economist, and used to go on walks during which the two of them would play chess games by visualising the moves.

But there were frustrations at Cambridge too. He had a rival: Maurice Wilkes had money and shared with Darwin the suspicion that Turing's minimalist design was allowing them to fall behind. Turing barely visited Wilkes' lab, though it was hardly far away; when he did he remarked that Wilkes looked like a beetle.

What Turing so badly needed was someone in authority who would recognise that the ridiculous, class-based division between theoreticians and engineers, which had made his work so frustrating at Teddington, ought to be dumped, and who was prepared to run with his vision of computing which was faster and simpler. It was as if, in order to create a vision of the split between hardware and software, he would have to end that same division among the pioneers of computing. It so happened that this was precisely the way forward, as understood by his old mentor Max Newman.

In May 1948 Turing resigned formally from the National Physical Laboratory. Darwin was furious, and Turing fulfilled his remaining obligations by writing one final report about intelligent machinery. The report listed the objections to intelligent machines. There was the limited ability of all machines so far produced, which was not encouraging. There was the fact that human beings can go beyond the failure of some machines to come up with answers. There was the problem that the 'intelligence' of machines might only be a reflection of the intelligence of their creators. There was also the 'unwillingness to admit that mankind can have any rivals in intellectual power', perhaps the core of the argument since.

Again, Turing seemed to be identifying with the machines which, although he had not created them yet, were in a sense his own creations. He wanted to give them the benefit of the doubt, because he believed they could be educated. Turing was aware that he was not trying to create a complete human being. He was not planning to create something with eyes and limbs. This was no robot he was planning; it was a *mind* – and it would be taught using the machine equivalent of pleasure and pain.

This is fascinating for so many reasons, not least of which is the way that the arguments have echoed down the decades ever since. Is there actually a machine equivalent of pleasure and pain? Is machine intelligence and human intelligence in any way related? But it is equally clear, reading the very personal arguments that Turing put forward, that the argument was at the core of his being. He identified with these educable machines, and with their ability to calculate the world in a logical way. It hardly needs saying that such machines would harbour no social aversion to men who loved men.

Turing seems to have seen his computers as having intelligent minds like his own. He identified with them, and his defence of them has sparked one of the great debates of the modern world – not so much 'can machines think', as it was articulated in the 1940s and 50s, but whether artificial intelligence was possible or meaningful – and what it might mean if these machines could go beyond human intelligence in the ways that Turing assumed, through translating, complex computing, playing chess.

Turing's report left these questions hanging, but he did suggest a forerunner of what would eventually become the Turing Test: if you played chess against a learning machine, would you know if it was a human being or a computer?

*

Newman's laboratory at Manchester University was more prosaic than King's College. It had hideous brown tiles. Turing rented rooms in Hale and then bought the only home he ever owned, in Adlington Road in Wilmslow, and cycled the twelve miles to the lab and back every day. His friendly neighbours, the Webbs, said he never took himself too seriously.

The machine he built with Newman was called Baby (officially, the Small-Scale Experimental Machine). It used Williams cathode ray tubes and indicated results in the form of lights. Turing wrote one of the first programmer's manuals, inventing a version of the Post Office's teleprinter code, with 32 numbers. It was extremely obscure and students complained that he never quite explained it in lectures.

In the background all the time was the newspaper and radio debate about 'electronic brains', a story which he had unintentionally begun himself. The MIT futurist Norbert Wiener sought him out, as many pioneers did, to discuss some of the implications for the future. Some of the scenarios felt like science fiction. All this came to the ears of Sir Geoffrey Jefferson, Professor of Neurosurgery and an advocate of frontal lobotomy. He was asked to give the Lister Oration in 1949 and called it 'The Mind of Mechanical Man', an attempt to debunk Turing's computer project:

'Not until a machine can write a sonnet or compose a concert because of thoughts and emotions felt, and not by the chance fall of symbolism, could we agree that machine equals brain – that isn't only to write it but know that it had written it.'

Jefferson was articulating the classic response to Turing, and it was even more uncomfortable that it got into the *Times*, which chose to ridicule Newman's funders at the Royal Society. A reporter contacted Turing and he found himself quoted in response: 'This is only a foretaste of what is to come, and only the shadow of what is going to be.'

The last quote had not been intended for publication at all. The sonnet comparison was unfair, he said. 'A sonnet written by a machine will be better appreciated by another machine.' His relatives remarked how like Alan this was, and this was his position: computers were like humans, and yet different – a class apart. Like Turing himself they could solve logical problem, but could not quite master the accepted codes of human interaction. Or could they?

*

The stage was set for Turing's most famous academic intervention. In October 1950, in the philosophical journal *Mind*, he published the article for which he remains so famous. He called it 'Computing machinery and intelligence'.

As he knew, he was wrestling with precisely the same question which had been tackled before the war by his old teacher, Wittgenstein, in precisely these words: can machines think? Wittgenstein had been sceptical, arguing that the problem lay in the word 'think'. If it meant just coming up with an answer to a set of questions, or working things out, then obviously machines can think – but if you mean something specifically human, then that becomes more complicated.

Most of the argument since, occasionally bitter, sometimes angry, has revolved around this. But Turing was about to become the symbolic hero of the academic movement that was to be known as artificial intelligence or AI. He has remained the hero because he proposed an experiment to resolve the question, as a mathematician might do, just as he had for his first academic paper about 'decidability' and the liar's paradox. He proposed an imitation game. There would be a man (A), a woman (B) and an interrogator (C) in a separate room, reading the written answers from the others, trying to work out which was the woman. B would be trying to hinder the process. Now, said Turing, imagine that A was replaced by a computer. Could the interrogator tell whether they were talking to a machine or not after five minutes of questioning?

He gave snatches of written conversation to show how difficult the Turing Test would be:

Q: Please write me a sonnet on the subject of the Forth Bridge.

A: Count me out on this one. I never could write poetry.

To imitate that a computer would need deep knowledge of social mores and the use of language. To pass the Turing Test the computer would have to do more than imitate. It would have to be a learning entity. But Turing also made a prediction:

'I believe that in about 50 years' time, it will be possible to produce computers, with a storage capacity of $[\![10]\!]$ $^\wedge(9$)to make them play the imitation game so well that an average interrogator will not have more than 70 per cent chance of making the right identification after five minutes of questioning.'

The *Mind* article has been one of the most debated academic contributions to philosophy of the century and has been subject to careful sceptical analysis. There have been suggestions that the whole business of distinguishing between a man and woman displays a strange, perhaps characteristic, sexual anxiety. Maybe it does, but it is precisely the way that Turing approached these and other matters – as a business of interpreting codes. In any case, the core of the article was whether it was possible between a human being and a machine.

He also exercised the various objections and, once again, defended the right of his machines to have human abilities and disabilities, to 'be kind, resourceful, beautiful, friendly, have initiative, have a sense of humour, tell right from wrong, make mistakes, fall in love, enjoy strawberries and cream...'

This was provocative stuff, as much about shocking the audience into understanding his message as it was about arguing the point. But his key argument was really about *consciousness*: it was not true that only humans could think because only humans were conscious. Here we really get to the nub of Turing's argument:

'This argument appears to be a denial of the validity of our test. According to the most extreme form of this view, the only way by which one could be sure that a machine thinks is to BE the machine and to feel oneself thinking.'

This is important. The argument since Turing has circled nervously around this question of whether machines can ever be complex enough to be conscious, and whether consciousness is uniquely human – and whether consciousness is a function of complexity anyway – though it is hard to see how computers could be friendly or kind without also being conscious.

The most enthusiastic advocates of AI certainly believe that we will eventually be able to download our brains onto computers. All this leads to much bigger questions, which we are really no closer to answering than Turing was, though there have been mathematical attempts to do so, notably by Turing's great disciple Roger Penrose.

But it also reveals Turing's own very English approach to the question. His intellectual development took place in the background of a philosophical doctrine which dominated debate in the 1930s, emerging out of the Vienna school and taking a distinctively English shape at the hands of the philosopher A. J. Ayer in Oxford. It was called Logical Positivism.

Positivism was about language and how it relates to the world. The positivists were also extreme empiricists. If there was no sense data to verify a sentence, then the sentence wasn't just wrong – it was meaningless. For example, the statement: 'Last night, everything in the universe doubled in size,' would have no meaning because it could not be checked one way or another. Positivists were flinging religious and moral statements into the bin.

Wittgenstein was contemptuous of positivism, but that was philosophical background to Turing's education. It was why they disagreed during their debates in King's. The Turing Test tries to make the whole question of thinking machines *decidable*.

Since 1941, according to his biographer Andrew Hodges, Turing had been watching his proto-computers and decided that originality and intuition were processes that could be computed. As a good positivist, Turing required no other data to explain creativity, and there was no sense data to suggest anything else was required. The Turing Test was simply an attempt to decide the issue one way or the other.

When would a machine be judged conscious? he joked. When it would punish you for saying otherwise. Turing thought in terms of tests like this.

Still, he made a friend of Jefferson. When Turing was made a fellow of the Royal Society in 1951 he got note of congratulations from his old sparring partner, saying: 'I sincerely trust that all your valves are glowing with satisfaction'. And during a broadcast on the BBC, Jefferson came up with his own test – which once again plunged the whole question of AI back into the realms of sex, from where it evidently emerged. He would not believe a machine could think 'until he saw it touch the leg of a lady computing machine'.

*

There was a strange humorous aside on the broadcast. '*Are* mathematicians human?' someone asks in the background. In fact, Turing was moving away from his interest in human beings, computing and AI and beginning to work on biological life. He wanted to know whether mathematical models lay behind biological processes. But his work was about to be overtaken by a personal disaster, a tragedy which seems to have led to the end of his brilliant life.

He was getting bolder in his sexual encounters. His friend Neville Johnson was away and Turing was increasingly in the habit of going abroad, where the atmosphere was more permissive, for his erotic adventures. In January 1952 he picked up a young man called Arnold Murray outside the Regal Cinema. Murray was 19 and short of money. Turing took him to lunch and invited him to his house for the weekend. He never showed up.

They met again and Murray did stay the night, but the relationship remained ambiguous. Murray refused to be paid but borrowed money. Turing sent him a penknife but also noticed that some other money was missing. A few days later his house was broken into and belongings were stolen. Turing called the police and they finger-printed the house. At the same time Turing wondered whether Murray had been involved somehow in the break-in and consulted his neighbour's solicitor. On advice he wrote to Murray, reminded him about the missing money, and suggested that it might be best if they didn't see each other again.

Murray was furious and came round to the house in a threatening mood. Later he admitted he had boasted about Turing to young man called Harry, who suggested they rob the house. Murray said he had refused to have anything to do with it and promised to try and get the stuff back. But by now the police had become suspicious and Turing and Murray were both arrested for gross indecency on 7 February 1952, the day that King George VI died and his daughter Elizabeth came to the throne. Turing was incredulous, complaining to the police – wrongly, in fact – that there was an official commission discussing repealing the law against homosexual acts. The trial took place at the end of March.

Both Turing and Murray pleaded guilty (Murray was defended by the future Liberal MP Emlyn Hooson, who went on to defend Moors murderer Ian Brady), but in the witness box Turing showed no remorse and pleaded no special circumstances – though Max Newman and other colleagues gave character evidence. 'The day of the trial was by no means disagreeable,' he wrote to a friend later. 'Whilst in custody with the other criminals I had a very agreeable sense of irresponsibility, rather like being at school.'

The judge decided not to send him to prison, but the sentence included a course of oestrogen treatment, intended to 'cure' him. It was a kind of chemical castration; it made him fat and made it difficult to concentrate. He grew breasts. No wonder letters to Robin Gandy talked about his 'shocking tendency at present to fritter my time away in anything but what I ought to be doing.' It was a terrible time, as he wrote to his friend Norman Routledge:

'I've now got myself into the kind of trouble that I have always considered to be quite a possibility for me.... the story of how it all came to be found out is a long and fascinating one, which I shall have to make into a short story one day, but have not time to tell now. No doubt I shall emerge from it all a different man, but quite who I've not found out.'

It was during this letter that his famous, despairing syllogism was included:

Turing believes machines think.

Turing lies with men.

Therefore machines cannot think.

He signed it: 'Yours in distress'. It meant, as he knew very well by then, not just the embarrassment of the revelation of his lifestyle to his family, but an end to all government code work. He had been helping with some of the efforts involved in cracking Soviet codes, and probably some of the calculations involved for nuclear weapons and nuclear energy. But not any more.

On the other hand, he was now interested in new fields, and it was a genuine pioneering interest, not an enforced shift as a result of the end of his previous work, though he was still on the staff at Manchester and protected by Newman. He became captivated by the mathematics of biology, publishing one paper on 'The Chemical Basis of Morphogenesis'. He was fascinated by how patterns emerge in nature – from zebra stripes to the patterns on flowers, and the link with the Fibonacci sequence. It was ground-breaking stuff and an early example of what would eventually emerge as chaos theory. Once more Turing was at the absolute cutting edge but, once more, also working on it alone.

During his two years of probation, and periods of deep introspection, he kept a dream diary and regularly saw a Jungian psychotherapist in Blackpool. He even wrote up the story of his encounter with Murray as a short story. The trouble was that the police were still watching him. This was not the local police, but other more shadowy intelligence organizations, aware that Turing knew a great deal.

His foreign expeditions also unnerved them. In the summer of 1953, Coronation year, he had a trip to Paris, to Corfu and another holiday to seek out the new gay movement in Norway. One Norwegian visitor who tried to visit him in the UK afterwards was sent home again by Special Branch.

'I've had another round with the gendarmes,' he wrote after that, 'and it's positively Round II to Turing... Being on probation, my shining virtue was terrific and had to be. If I had so much as parked my bicycle on the wrong side of the road there might have been 12 years for me. Of course the police are going to be a bit more nosy, so virtue must continue to shine.'

*

But time was running out for Turing. During Christmas 1953 his mother warned him about his chemical experiments at home, and to be careful to wash his hands. 'I'm not going to injure myself, mother,' he replied. His biographer Andrew Hodges believes that this may have provided the spark of an idea for what he saw as a way out.

As it turned out later, his mood was uncertain. On a trip to the seaside at Blackpool with the family of his therapist, Franz Greenbaum, there was a fortune teller's tent on the promenade. It is an old cliché, his therapist's daughter remembered Turing going in and coming out some time later ashen-faced. He never said what had happened, and we only have the daughter's word for this uncomfortable but uncategorizable incident.

Robin Gandy spent the weekend with Turing at the end of May 1954, and they carried out chemical experiments in the little laboratory he had rigged up next to his bedroom. Shortly afterwards he invited his neighbour Mrs Webb in for tea and she described him as 'full of plans'. Another weekend went by until his housekeeper Mrs Clayton returned on the morning of 8 June and saw his bedroom light on, his curtains still closed and his milk and newspaper uncollected.

She assumed he had gone out early, knocked at his bedroom door and, when there was no answer, she walked in. Turing was dead. He was lying prone in bed and, beside the bed, was an apple with several bites taken out of it. 'It was such an awful shock. I just didn't know what to do,' Mrs Clayton told his mother later.

The inquest two days later decided a verdict of suicide. He was cremated at Woking Crematorium.

The autopsy report suggested that he had drunk about four ounces of cyanide. It was assumed that there had been some of this on the apple, though this was never tested. It seems more likely that he drank some and then ate the apple to give some evidence to his mother that this had been an accident. Certainly, Sara Turing believed that until she died in 1976. Her memoir of her son, published in 1959, is full of testimony to his achievements and brilliance, though Alan's brother John claims that she did not see him in quite that light while he was alive. We will never know for certain.

VII

'Don't ever ask what the war was for – it's hush-hush.'
Julian Slade and Dorothy Reynolds, *Salad Days*,
1954

Early in June 1951, while Turing was working in Manchester (and by which time IBM had 30,000 employees), an abandoned car was discovered in the car park at Southampton Docks. The man who had hired it had apparently shouted at staff that he would be back the following week. In fact, he never returned: his name was Guy Burgess.

Burgess and his friend Donald Maclean were both Soviet agents and had disappeared on the advice of their contact at MI6, Kim Philby, the so-called Third Man. Ironically it was the interception of coded signals which had begun the hunt for Maclean. A copy of a telegram between Prime

Minister Winston Churchill and President Harry Truman had been sent to Moscow, presumably via a copy found at the British embassy in Washington. It became clear that the same mole, nicknamed HOMER, had also met his Soviet handler regularly in Washington too. The finger was increasingly pointing towards Maclean.

Burgess was flamboyantly homosexual. Maclean was described in his Foreign Office files as a repressed homosexual. Homosexuality was about to feature at the very top of the security panic that was to follow. It was no coincidence that the fall-out from Burgess and Maclean happened in parallel with the unravelling of Turing's official career. His biographer Andrew Hodges implies there is a link with his death, but none of his biographers have really been able to spell out what the link was.

The question of precisely why Turing died at the early age of 41 has been complicated by the debate about whether this was indeed suicide, or whether it was accidental death. There have inevitably been dark internet rumours that he was in some way 'disposed of' by the authorities. There is no evidence for this. Quite the reverse: the manner of his death, if it was not an accident, was so personal and idiosyncratic, that it is extremely hard to imagine anyone else devising it. Hodges also suggests that Turing chose this particular means of killing himself – not for its symbolic value, as some biographers claim – but because it was an ingenious way of hiding the fact that this was suicide from his mother. She had warned him only months before about the dangers of his chemical experiments.

Whatever the truth, this was certainly the effect it had. Sara Turing was convinced that this was an unfortunate accident. Her memoir of his life devotes a good third of the book to evidence from friends that he had no intention of killing himself. She quotes Greenbaum, his psychotherapist, from a letter saying that 'there is not the slightest doubt to me that Alan died by an accident'.

The argument emerged again thanks to Hodges' rival, Professor Jack Copeland, director of the Turing archive, who argued in 2012 that a modern court would never have reached a suicide verdict, especially as the apple was never actually tested for cyanide. This is true, but the circumstantial evidence is actually quite strong. Turing's body lay comfortably in bed: it did not look like an accidental death. He had recently made a will. Also Greenbaum had not been quite honest with Sara Turing and, when he lent his patient's dream diaries to Turing's brother John, it convinced John that this was, in fact, a case of suicide. It almost certainly was.

The real question then is *why*, given that he had ended his hormone treatment and was making some progress in new fields like morphology. Turing knew that his government career had ended, including any work that he had been doing for GCHQ. He expected no great change in the climate of opinion. He was supported in Manchester by Newman and some close friends, and may not have expected any opportunities for new work. There was also the strange story about the abortive visit of his Norwegian friend Kjell in 1953.

This is how Hodges set it out:

'Turing never fully explained this crisis about Kjell, the young Norwegian, but told Robin later that "for sheer incident" it rivalled the arrest and trial in 1952. Kjell had arrived at Newcastle from Norway, and police ("the poor sweeties" as Turing called them) were watching his house, and were deployed all over the North of England to intercept him.'

Why were Special Branch officers deployed all over northern England to head off Kjell? The answer lies in the strange paranoia of the time. Thanks to help from the Manchester computer project, the first British nuclear bomb was tested in October 1952. The first Soviet hydrogen bomb was tested in August 1953. There was another American H-bomb test in March 1954. The Cold War was cooling rapidly and Turing seems to have been involved in some of the top secret mathematics.

The defection of Burgess and Maclean led to a serious panic inside the UK security services, driven in part by the furious Americans who – under the influence of Senator Joe McCarthy and his anti-communist crusade – had serious doubts about whether their secrets were safe with the British. In 1952 the UK government decided on a deep in-depth investigation into the lives and backgrounds of people before appointing them to sensitive positions. Positive vetting was introduced as part of a deal between Britain, France and the USA. It was widely acknowledge that vetting had to go beyond communist sympathies, and go into what the report official report into the Burgess and Maclean affair called 'character defects' – failings such as 'drunkenness, addiction to drugs, homosexuality, or any loose living'.

'It is right to continue the practice of tilting the balance in favour of offering greater protection to the security of the state, rather than in the direction of safeguarding the rights of the individual,' said the same report.

The process was described in more detail in an MI5 booklet published in 1964, ten years after Turing's death, and distributed to civil servants.

'Spies are with us all the time,' it said. 'This booklet tells you about the great hostile spy machine that tries to suborn our citizens and turn them into traitors.'

Hodges hints at the crisis, explaining that Turing's holidays in Norway and Greece in 1953, dangerously near the Iron Curtain, could 'not have been calculated to calm the nerves of security officers'. That must be an understatement. He goes onto describe Turing's summer holiday in the summer of 1953 as an 'act of defiance', which may have led to interrogations. There is no way of knowing exactly what prompted Turing's death, but we can be reasonably sure that the security services were extremely worried about him. It was already clear how vital computing was to cryptography and for speeding up the exhausting calculations for nuclear weaponry. Turing was probably the leading theoretician in this field in the world. He had deep knowledge of the efforts to crack Nazi codes in wartime, on both sides of the Atlantic, which remained highly secret until the 1970s.

If the British were relaxed about the possibility of his defection, knowing that he had almost no interest in politics, then the Americans would not be. The pressure on the British was huge. Not only could they not risk losing Turing, they could not be seen to be risking losing him. Something had to be done to rein him in. Yet, what hold could they have over someone like Turing to prevent him wandering abroad and getting into compromising situations? Cancelling his security clearance would not help. Nor would appealing to his better nature. Nor would close surveillance, which we know he was under for this period.

They could remove his passport, but that might have had the effect of precipitating exactly the crisis they feared most. They must have known about his sexual adventures – a list of the men Turing had met abroad was shown to Andrew Hodges in 1978 before it was destroyed by what he called a 'censorious employee of the Atomic Weapons Research Establishment'.

Was it possible that the security services were so worried about his next summer holiday (it was June) that they threatened to show the list to his mother? Did they threaten to remove him from his academic posts? Did they threaten to prosecute him if he went abroad again? We have no idea, but something may have pushed Turing over the edge. He felt certain that his computers would be able to think and feel, but he had no idea if the regime that was paying him such close attention – with its fierce horror of homosexuality – would last forever.

Turing has been portrayed as a victim of sexual intolerance. He certainly was, but – as Hodges hints so eloquently in his biography, without quite spelling it out – he was also a victim of the Cold War.

*

In 2003 one of the American pioneers of artificial intelligence, Marvin Minksy, dismissed the movement which had been trying to progress towards the goals set out by Turing half a century before. 'AI has been brain-dead since the 1970s,' he said. 'For each different kind of problem, the construction of expert systems had to start all over again, because they didn't accumulate common-sense knowledge.... Graduate students are wasting three years of their lives soldering and repairing robots, instead of making them smart. It's really shocking.'

AI is supposed to have burst into the academic world in 1956, but this is a heroic American view. Turing was deeply involved in the debate and practicalities during the Second World War. But it is the USA which really took AI to his heart. It is hardly surprising that it was there that the American inventor Hugh Loebner made the first really concerted attempt to encourage engineers to take the Turing Test, offering a prize of $100,000 to anyone who could build a computer that could pass it.

The Loebner Prize Competition in Artificial Intelligence took place for the first time in 1991 in Boston, with the philosopher Daniel Dennett chairing the judging panel. Dennett pointed out the immediate problem, which was that Turing's test was extremely tough and there was absolutely no chance that any existing computer was going to pass it. So he lowered the bar. There were ten judges and ten terminals and they would all spend fifteen minutes with each terminal. Six would be computers and four would be human and the judges would have to work out which. Even then, Dennett did not expect to have to hand out any prizes.

He lost his nerve during the actual judging and went to the office to knock-up a certificate just in case. In the event, he gave out three. 'The gullibility of the judges was simply astonishing to me. How *could* they have misjudged so badly?' he wrote. Often, as it turned out, they were simply doing what Turing suggested and giving the machines the benefit of the doubt.

Dennett went on to suggest this question:

'An Irishman found a genie in a bottle who offered him two wishes. "First, I'll have a pint of Guinness," said the Irishman, and when it appeared he took several long drinks from it and was delighted to see that the glass filled itself magically as he drank. "What about your second wish?" asked the genie. "Oh well," said the Irishman, "that's easy. I'll have another one of these!" Please explain this story to me, and tell me if there is anything funny or sad about it.'

Dennett said that if a computer could genuinely answer this question to the satisfaction of a human interrogator, then yes, you could certainly say it could think. It is still unclear whether that will ever happen.

The whole question of thinking machines remains deeply controversial, and rightly so, because these are questions about the nature of humanity. The roots of the Turing Test in logical positivism and English philosophy is part of the problem. Turing was trying to find a way – not to decide the nature of humanity but whether machines could think. He saw no real distinction between whether the computer could fool an interrogator that it was human and whether it was *actually* thinking.

In 1980 the English philosopher John Searle published his assault in an important philosophical article. It included with a story called 'The Chinese Room'. Imagine a sealed room with a man who doesn't understand Chinese inside, said Searle. Imagine he gets messages in Chinese, looks them up in a lexicon and finds them associated with other Chinese characters, which he passes back – without knowing that the messages he is getting are questions and the messages he is sending are answers. Now, the man might be able to convince the equivalent of Turing's interrogator that he could understand Chinese, but actually he couldn't.

However accurate the man's translation proves, can we say that he *understands* Chinese, asks Searle. The answer, he says, is no. 'It is not easy for me to imagine how someone who was not in the grip of an ideology would find the idea at all plausible,' wrote Searle. Once again, the question came down to the meanings of words: in what sense do we mean that the computer can 'understand'? In

Turing's narrow sense, or in Searle's more metaphysical sense?

Searle was right about ideology. There is a kind of AI ideology that is claiming much more for the Turing Test than it can quite withstand. These are 'born again' positivists, seeing themselves as making a stand for rationality, when actually they may just be in the middle of an unanswered philosophical conundrum, based on the rival meaning of the words like 'think', 'intelligent' and 'human'.

On the one hand, there are true believers like Ray Kurzweil, the author of *The Age of Spiritual Machines*. On the other hand, there are critics like Jaron Lanier, the pioneer of virtual reality. 'Turing assumed that the computer in this case [having passed the Test] has become smarter or more humanlike,' he told the *New York Times*. 'But the equally likely conclusion is that the person has become dumber and more computerlike.'

The British critic Bryan Appleyard wrote a similar critique of the ideology in his book *The Brain is*

Wider Than the Sky, where he says that the arguments for replacing human functions with IT are often based on narrow assumptions of what can be achieved by human intelligence and intuition.

But the victory of IBM's Big Blue computer over chess champion Garry Kasparov in 1997does imply that a shift has happened. Both human genetics and AI try to reduce human life in some way to numbers, and both are stuck and may in fact be looking in the wrong direction. But it is absolutely clear that computers have long since surpassed human computation abilities; there are some things that computers will do far better than humans.

There seems to be a broader debate emerging about what it means to be human in the light of the Turing Test. The Turing Test never claimed to be able to verify anything metaphysical, but that is where the debate is going. It is a debate about authenticity, which asserts or denies that there are attributes which are uniquely human, not so much conventional intelligence, but love, care and generosity. Turing believed that intuition was computable. Even if a computer passes his test, we won't know if he was right or not.

Turing was wrong about his predictions: he expected his test to have been passed by now. But we are now in thrall to computers in ways that might have surprised him: in practice, the closer to human intelligence the robot who phones us up can be, the more unnerving the experience – and, for the time being, the more frustrating, because of the inability of information technology to deal with human complexity in the ways that Turing predicted. If the corporate world wants to replace teachers and doctors with screens and software because it is cheaper, it is not always obvious which side Turing – a great humanist – would have been on.

*

It is never entirely comfortable when a complex human being becomes a symbol of things beyond themselves. Turing has become a symbol for the modern world, as a prophet of information technology and scientific rationality, a martyr for gay rights, and also a genius cramped by convention and intolerance.

He would have found none of these entirely comfortable. He is portrayed sometimes as a social misfit somewhere on the autistic spectrum – in fact he was a witty and entertaining friend. He was, in fact, a far more rounded figure than he is given credit for being. As for the symbolism of the apple, it is a bizarre twist of the modern world that Turing's fatal apple is sometimes given the credit for being the original for the logo which now graces Apple computers – as if the apple of the tree of knowledge was somehow inadequate to the task.

In fact, the Apple logo's designer Rob Janoff denies that he had even Adam and Eve in mind when he penned his first draft. He put the bite in, not as a tribute to Turing, but to emphasise scale and to show this was not a picture of a cherry.

Either way, Turing's reputation is growing. Back in 1999 *Time* magazine named him as one of the 100 most important people of the twentieth century. In the centenary of his birth there were celebratory events in more than 40 countries. There was an exhibition in the Science Museum in London and a commemorative stamp issued by the Royal Mail. His universal computer was voted the greatest British invention of the twentieth century.

Lord Sharkey's new law was pre-empted by the government just before Christmas 2013, afraid of the precedent it would set if it passed. So Turing got his posthumous pardon anyway, yet the turn-out by some of the most eminent men and women of science for the debate five months before was a sign of how Turing's reputation had soared since his death.

'There is now a statue of Turing in Manchester, where he lived, worked and died,' Lord Sharkey told the House of Lords in July 2013. 'There is now a statue of Turing in Paddington, where he lived for a while. The statue stands alongside statues of Mary Seacole and Paddington Bear. All three statues were voted for by the residents and it strikes me as a peculiarly and encouragingly British set of choices.'

Then Lord Quirk, the famous linguist, rose to reply. 'I end by noting something surely perverse, if constitutionally sound enough, about this bill,' he said. 'It would grant Alan a pardon, when surely all of us would far prefer to receive a pardon from him.'

Bibliography

Alan Turing homepage www.turing.org.uk (updated by Andrew Hodges); some of his letters are included at www.turingarchive.org.

Briggs, Asa (2011), *Secret Days*: *Code breaking in Bletchley Park*, London: Frontline.

Copeland, Jack (ed.) (2002), *The Essential Turing*, Oxford: Oxford University Press.

Diamond, Cora (ed.) (1976), *Wittgenstein's Lectures on the Foundations of Mathematics, Cambridge 1939*, Hassocks: Harvester Press.

Eldridge, Jim (2013), *Alan Turing*, London: Bloomsbury/Real Lives.

Goldstein, Rebecca (2005), *Incompleteness*: *The proof and paradox of Kurt Godel*, New York: Norton.

Hodges, Andrew (2000), *Alan Turing*: *The Enigma*, New York: Walker Books.

Leavitt, David (2006), *The Man Who Knew Too Much*: *Alan Turing and the invention of the computer*, London: Weidenfeld & Nicolson.

McKay, Sinclair (2010), *The Secret Life of Bletchley Park*, London: Aurum Press.

Penrose, Roger (1999), *The Emperor's New Mind*: *Concerning computers, minds and the laws of physics*, Oxford: Oxford University Press.

Searle, John (1984), *Minds, Brains and Science*, Cambridge MA: Harvard University Press.

Teuscher, Christof (ed.) (2004), *Alan Turing*: *Life and legacy of a great thinker*, Berlin: Springer.

Turing, Sara (1959), *Alan M. Turing*, Cambridge: Heffer & Co.

Acknowledgements

I am enormously grateful for the help and advice I have received during the writing of this book, especially from Richard Foreman, who is always a store of good advice, and from my agent Julian Alexander. I was also given invaluable guidance about the mathematics by Mark Treveil and by John Sharkey, which made some of the darkness light. But any mistakes are mine alone.

About the Author

David Boyle is a fellow of the New Economics Foundation, and the author of a number of books about economics, business and the future, as well as history, including *Blondel's Song* and *Toward the Setting Sun*, about the discovery of America. He also writes widely about new thinking, including his books *The Age to Come* and *Authenticity*. www.david-boyle.co.uk.

18873523R10065

Made in the USA
San Bernardino, CA
01 February 2015